A Joy to Behold

Rediscovering Delight in the Christmas Season

A 15-Day Advent Devotional

TARYN NERGAARD

typewriter
creative co.

© 2020 Taryn Nergaard

www.tarynnergaard.com

All rights reserved. This book or any portion thereof may not be reproduced or used in any manner whatsoever without the express written permission of the publisher except for the use of brief quotations.

Cover & interior design by Typewriter Creative Co.
Cover photo by Joanna Kosinska on Unsplash.com.

Unless otherwise noted, all Scripture quotations are taken from the Christian Standard Bible® Copyright © 2017 by Holman Bible Publishers. Used by permission. Christian Standard Bible®, and CSB® are federally registered trademarks of Holman Bible Publishers.

Scripture quotations marked (NIV) are taken from the Holy Bible, New International Version®, NIV®. Copyright © 1973, 1978, 1984, 2011 by Biblica, Inc.™ Used by permission of Zondervan. All rights reserved worldwide. www.zondervan.comThe "NIV" and "New International Version" are trademarks registered in the United States Patent and Trademark Office by Biblica, Inc.™

ISBN 978-1-7770331-5-6 (Paperback)
ISBN 978-1-7770331-6-3 (eBook)

Don't be afraid, for look, I proclaim to you good news of great joy that will be for all the people: Today in the city of David a Savior was born for you, who is the Messiah, the Lord.

LUKE 2:10-11

CONTENTS

Introduction 7
One 9
Two 11
Three 13
Four 15
Five 17
Six 19
Seven 21
Eight 23
Nine 25
Ten 27
Eleven 29
Twelve 31
Thirteen 33
Fourteen 35
Fifteen 37
A Final Note 39
About the Author 41

INTRODUCTION

I named this devotional *A Joy to Behold* for two reasons:

First, our Lord Jesus Christ is a joy to behold. His birth, his life, his death, and his resurrection all display a story that is miraculous and magnificent. When we allow ourselves to step into his story we can't help but be filled with wonder at all he has done for us.

Second, joy is yours to hold if you'll accept it. It isn't dependent on our circumstances, nor is it dependent on our feelings or our pain. We can learn to hold fast to joy even when the storms of life rage around us.

I pray these short reflections help you to calm the chaos, quiet your soul, and rediscover the delight of the season.

I'm with you.

ONE

GALATIANS 6:9-10 (NIV)

Let us not become weary in doing good, for at the proper time we will reap a harvest if we do not give up. Therefore, as we have opportunity, let us do good to all people, especially to those who belong to the family of believers.

If the enemy can't take you out, he'll steal your joy.

That's the whisper of God I heard in December 2017 during another busy Christmas season. It wasn't long before I discovered God hadn't only revealed that truth for my own heart, but for many others in my life. As Christmas Eve approached, I had the opportunity to speak to several women of varying ages who felt weary and run-down with all the holiday preparations. The common thread that wove between the frazzled women was that they'd lost the joy in doing good.

There weren't more responsibilities or expectations than the previous years, yet this year they felt undone because the joy of the season was no longer held deeply within their souls. Without joy, we cannot rise above the overwhelm.

The good work for which we are called weighs heavy on us, and we feel like giving up.

As you read this, it's likely only the beginning of December. But now is the best time to make a decision about how we will approach the holiday season. Let's decide here and now that we're going to enter this season with a firm grasp on joy. For when we have joy, we have the power to persevere.

PRAYER

God, I know what this season is truly about. I know that this month we get to celebrate the birth of your son, and our saviour, Jesus Christ. That reason alone should be enough to fill my heart with joy and excitement, yet I know that it can be easy to forget. Please help me to stay focused on the gift of Jesus as the reason for all our celebrations. Help me also to have a glad heart as I look for ways to glorify you in all my preparations and plans. Thank you for showing love to me by sending your son to Earth. I want to show my love to you by honoring that gift this month. Amen.

TWO

ISAIAH 63:7

I will make known the Lord's faithful love and the Lord's praiseworthy acts, because of all the Lord has done for us—even the many good things he has done for the house of Israel, which he did for them based on his compassion and the abundance of his faithful love.

Do you "make known the Lord's faithful love" in your life? Gratitude is the key that unlocks the door to joy, and our God has given us an infinite measure of things for which to be grateful. Being busy can cause us to become so distracted by our daily tasks that we forget to notice all the good things God gives us each day.

As we look to develop a deep sense of joy this month, gratitude must become a daily, habitual practice. How you tune your mind and heart towards God's faithfulness is up to you, but here are a few examples of ways we can be intentional about finding good in every day:

1. Keep an index card in your pocket so that every time you feel it there, you'll remember to pull it out and write down

something you are grateful for in that moment.

2. Start your day by journaling. Thank God for the ways you know he will be good to you that day, even before you know what circumstances you will face.

3. At the end of each day, make a list of 5 specific ways you experienced God's goodness in your day.

PRAYER

God, I know you are good. You have been faithful to me even when I have not acknowledged it. I want to be more intentional about noticing all the good things in my day so that I have a heart filled with gratitude instead of grumbling. Help me to see my life through new eyes this month so that I can celebrate with joy and thanksgiving all that you've done for me. Amen.

THREE

JOHN 15:1-5

I am the true vine, and my Father is the gardener. Every branch in me that does not produce fruit he removes, and he prunes every branch that produces fruit so that it will produce more fruit. You are already clean because of the word I have spoken to you. Remain in me, and I in you. Just as a branch is unable to produce fruit by itself unless it remains on the vine, neither can you unless you remain in me. I am the vine; you are the branches. The one who remains in me and I in him produces much fruit, because you can do nothing without me.

How often do we overestimate ourselves? I know I do. I see the evidence of my pride when I say yes when my schedule is already full. I see it when I deny myself time with God because there are more urgent things to do.

We often think we are much more capable than we are. We fail to realize this simple truth: we need God. No, we *desperately* need God. Yet we don't always act like it, do we? We keep trying and trying and trying on our own instead of taking the time to connect with God—our true source of strength and our greatest helper.

This December, let's stop rushing ahead on our own and let's hold onto God with everything, knowing that he is the source of all that we need for each day.

PRAYER

Lord, thank you for always being near to me. I admit that I struggle to stay connected to you some days. Instead of asking for your help, I rush ahead to do it all on my own. But my way often leaves me feeling exhausted and inadequate. Please help me to slow down and recognize your presence and strength throughout my day. Amen.

FOUR

LAMENTATIONS 3:22-24

Because of the Lord's faithful love we do not perish, for his mercies never end. They are new every morning; great is your faithfulness! I say, "The Lord is my portion, therefore I will put my hope in him."

To lament means to mourn or express sorrow. I know that someone reading this devotional today will have an intimate, present understanding of the word. The truth is, the longer we live, the more opportunities we have to experience heartbreaking sorrow. It's the reality of our world as mortal human beings who experience sickness and death.

But just as we experience more opportunities to lament, so also we experience more opportunities to experience the never-ending mercies of our Lord. Joy and sorrow are not mutually exclusive; they are mutually experienced. The tension between the two emotions is often where we learn a deeper, richly beautiful understanding of God's faithfulness.

Jesus' birth and—even more evidently—his death, bore

both joy and sorrow, yet God's mercy was never greater than in those moments of history. So, take heart today. You need not choose between joy and sorrow. You can lament the pain of this world and still hold firmly to the hope of God's faithful love for you.

PRAYER

Lord Jesus, you are my strength and my shield, my ever-present help in times of trouble. I know that I can persevere with your help. Thank you for your faithfulness. Thank you that your love for me never fails. I will fix my eyes on you this season and see your mercy in each new day. Amen.

FIVE

PHILIPPIANS 2:1-4

If then there is any encouragement in Christ, if any consolation of love, if any fellowship with the Spirit, if any affection and mercy, make my joy complete by thinking the same way, having the same love, united in spirit, intent on one purpose. Do nothing out of selfish ambition or conceit, but in humility consider others as more important than yourselves. Everyone should look out not only for his own interests, but also for the interests of others.

I think we've all heard the Golden Rule, right? "Do to others as you would have them do to you." Or as I paraphrase to my kids: "Treat others the way you would like to be treated." While you may have heard it a hundred times before, I would like to suggest a different way of applying it.

This holiday season, instead of being disappointed by our unmet expectations of what we hope other people will do for us, let's go first.

If you wish that a friend would call you to meet for coffee—

call her first. If you're hoping to receive Christmas cards from friends and family—send out cards yourself. If you have your eye on a particularly special Christmas gift—purchase gifts for others that you know will bring them joy.

What you'll notice when you go first is that your own longings are partially, or even fully, met by the act of doing something for someone else. By focusing on the needs of others and bringing joy to their lives, we end up feeling most satisfied.

PRAYER

God, thank you for giving me grace when I start grumbling about what I don't have. Help me to pass along that grace to others this season as I look for ways to love and serve those around me. Jesus, you are the ultimate example of what it means to "go first" and be a humble servant. Please help me to see other people the way you see them so that I can shift my focus from myself and better love the people in my family and community. Amen.

SIX

GALATIANS 3:27-29

For those of you who were baptized into Christ have been clothed with Christ. There is no Jew or Greek, slave or free, male and female; since you are all one in Christ Jesus. And if you belong to Christ, then you are Abraham's seed, heirs according to the promise.

I said earlier that Satan's goal is to steal your joy. Want to know his game plan?

Comparison.

There's no version of the comparison game that ends with a winner. Everyone loses. The Christmas season can bring out the worst in us and comparison is one reason why.

We look at her family and think they must be so happy because they can all be together for Christmas. We look at her house and think her life must be perfect because her house is perfectly decorated. We look at her body and think that it must be easier to handle all the holiday parties because she's thin and doesn't struggle with food.

This comparison game diminishes our ability to experience joy in what we have and pushes us to isolate ourselves from others. Instead of being "one in Christ Jesus" as the verse says, we become lonely and disconnected from the body of believers. Our isolation renders us unable to fulfill the purpose God has for us.

If we want to experience a meaningful Christmas, we must learn to see one another with eyes of unity instead of comparison. This starts with being deeply rooted in God's love and confident in his unique design for each of us.

PRAYER

God, please help me to see the people around me as brothers and sisters in Christ. Help me to see the ways in which comparison has separated me from the body of believers. I long to live a life of purpose and meaning and I understand that I'm not meant to live the Christian life alone. Please give me strength to stand firm in my identity instead of falling into the temptation to compare and judge. Amen.

SEVEN

PSALM 59:16-17

But I will sing of your strength and will joyfully proclaim your faithful love in the morning. For you have been a stronghold for me, a refuge in my day of trouble. To you, my strength, I sing praises, because God is my stronghold—my faithful God.

What we believe about God will shape how we respond to the circumstances of life. And right now, what we believe about God is shaping how we experience Christmas.

Do we believe that God is good and kind? Do we believe that every experience in our lives can be turned into a gift in his hands?

If you're struggling today to believe that God is good and kind, you need to slow down and start paying more attention to what is around you. And are you practicing gratitude each day like I talked about on Day Two?

If you look for ways that God is showing you his goodness, you'll keep seeing it everywhere. There is no shortage of reasons to sing and praise and joyfully proclaim the faithfulness of our God.

Life can seem difficult and dark when we're in the middle of the valley, but even there God is present. Look and you will find him.

PRAYER

God, I'm just trying to get through each day, and I don't know if I believe there really is good in every day. But I want to believe you are always good and always kind, so I will start looking. Help me to see you in all the little moments of my day. Help me to hope for better days to come. Amen.

EIGHT

ISAIAH 53

Yet he himself bore our sicknesses, and he carried our pains; but we in turn regarded him stricken, struck down by God, and afflicted. But he was pierced because of our rebellion, crushed because of our iniquities; punishment for our peace was on him, and we are healed by his wounds. We all went astray like sheep; we all have turned to our own way; and the Lord has punished him for the iniquity of us all.

We know that when we accept Jesus as our Lord and Savior we are saved from death into eternal life in heaven. Our souls were lost, but now they are found in Christ.

I'm not sure if you can relate to this or not, but sometimes I still get a bit lost. I don't lose faith, and I know that my eternal future is secure—yet I can step a little off course from time to time. I become a wandering sheep who strays a bit too far away from my Shepherd.

When my daily decisions start to follow my own way instead of God's way, I lose the feeling of safety that I feel when I stay directly under God's care. Jesus Christ is the Prince of Peace, and I have found there is no peace like that of a heart surrendered to him.

This Christmas, as we're busying ourselves in preparation for our Lord's birth, let's not take our eyes away from our Good Shepherd. Self-sufficiency leaves us feeling lost and anxious, but surrender fills us with peace and purpose.

PRAYER

God, thank you for being my Good Shepherd. Your ways are better than my ways, and when I trust you to guide me, I can handle life's circumstances so much better. I want to experience a deeper feeling of peace and rest this Christmas rather than getting swept up in the hurry and chaos. Jesus, thank you for taking the punishment I deserved so that I can live with peace here on earth and experience eternal pleasure in heaven with you one day. Amen.

NINE

PSALM 100

Let the whole earth shout triumphantly to the Lord! Serve the Lord with gladness; come before him with joyful songs. Acknowledge that the Lord is God. He made us, and we are his—his people, the sheep of his pasture. Enter his gates with thanksgiving and his courts with praise. Give thanks to him and bless his name. For the Lord is good, and his faithful love endures forever; his faithfulness, through all generations.

Can I let you in on a little secret? I love snow and Christmas music. Why is that a secret? Because all my life I lived with someone who has been a little more Scrooge than Buddy the Elf. My preferences melded into those around me, so I thought that because the people I love don't like snow or Christmas music or decorating before December 1st, then I must not like those things either.

Is there an area of your life that you're holding back from fully expressing your delight?

Maybe you don't like wearing your favourite cross necklace at work because you might be judged by your coworkers. Maybe you feel awkward having worship music on in your house because you have a houseguest who isn't a Christian. Maybe the people around you are all "bah humbug" about Christmas, and it's preventing you from enjoying the holiday season yourself.

Whatever it is that brings you joy and glorifies God, I want you to embrace it this month. Be confidently, unashamedly YOU. You may find yourself overflowing with so much joy and gladness that it spreads to those around you.

PRAYER

God, help me to see the unique way you made me and be confident in my identity. Help me to recognize what makes me joyful and find ways to embrace those things in my life, even if they seem odd or silly to others. Thank you for making me on purpose, with a purpose, and for a purpose. I'm grateful for everything you have given me, and I want to use it all for your glory. Amen.

TEN

1 THESSALONIANS 5:12-15 (NIV)

Now we ask you, brothers and sisters, to acknowledge those who work hard among you, who care for you in the Lord and who admonish you. Hold them in the highest regard in love because of their work. Live in peace with each other. And we urge you, brothers and sisters, warn those who are idle and disruptive, encourage the disheartened, help the weak, be patient with everyone. Make sure that nobody pays back wrong for wrong, but always strive to do what is good for each other and for everyone else.

We see consumerism as a problem of our culture during this time of the year, but it's also a problem in the church. We can easily fall into a "takers" mindset that sees everything through the lens of "what's in it for me?"

When we start seeing our church through that lens, we can become resentful, burned out, and disillusioned. We start to see all the ways that the church isn't meeting our needs instead of looking for ways we can meet the needs of others.

As my own pastor says, "The church isn't a 'what,' it's a 'who.' The church is me and the church is you."

If we see needs among ourselves that are not being met then we need to meet them. We also need to continually pray for our brothers and sisters in Christ, including the leaders of our church who are often carrying heavier burdens than we can imagine. Instead of pointing our finger at the gaps we see, let's be the ones who fill the gaps. Quietly, humbly, and joyfully we can follow Jesus' lead to serve, not be served.

PRAYER

Lord, please help me to follow the example of Jesus. If anyone deserves to be served, it's him, yet he came to love and serve us. Thank you for sending your son as a sacrifice so that I can live fully. Help me not to take that gift for granted and instead look for ways to show grace to others. Thank you for my pastors and church leaders. I ask that you strengthen them during this season, and show me ways that I can love and serve them well. Amen.

ELEVEN

1 PETER 4:12-16

Dear friends, don't be surprised when the fiery ordeal comes among you to test you as if something unusual were happening to you. Instead, rejoice as you share in the sufferings of Christ, so that you may also rejoice with great joy when his glory is revealed. If you are ridiculed for the name of Christ, you are blessed, because the Spirit of glory and of God rests on you. Let none of you suffer as a murderer, a thief, an evildoer, or a meddler. But if anyone suffers as a Christian, let him not be ashamed but let him glorify God in having that name.

I had this funny thought the other day that Christmas is like a massive birthday party where all these extra people show up, even though they don't know whose party it is. They're just there to have a good time. It's the friends of the birthday boy/girl who really know why they are there.

We know who we are celebrating at Christmas. And we know who we love, follow, and surrender our lives to daily.

It's that truth that allows us to face the "fiery ordeals" that come our way. We know that we don't suffer as a punishment but as refinement. Holding on to the truth of who we are—because of who Christ is—allows us to face hardship with peace and joy.

Unbelievers will have a difficult time understanding our way of living and our way of reacting to life's circumstances. But remember: we know who the party is for. We know who is worth celebrating and following with our whole hearts.

PRAYER

God, thank you for making yourself known to me and for providing your son Jesus so that I can have a personal relationship with you. So many people are celebrating something this season, yet I know that you are the one worth giving everything for. Thank you for this time to celebrate the ultimate gift of your Son. I never want to forget what that sacrifice means for me. Amen.

TWELVE

COLOSSIANS 3:12-15

Therefore, as God's chosen ones, holy and dearly loved, put on compassion, kindness, humility, gentleness, and patience, bearing with one another and forgiving one another if anyone has a grievance against another. Just as the Lord has forgiven you, so you are also to forgive. Above all, put on love, which is the perfect bond of unity. And let the peace of Christ, to which you were also called in one body, rule your hearts. And be thankful.

I don't believe it's possible to be thankful and bitter at the same time. Maybe that's why the holidays can be so painful. We are often placed in situations during the holidays that bring us face-to-face with people who have hurt us. When we have not dealt with our bitterness by forgiving others, the feelings of joy and gladness that seem to come easily for others at Christmas will continue to elude us.

The greatest gift you can give yourself this Christmas is the gift of forgiveness. Forgive yourself for whatever you're still holding against yourself. Forgive the people who have hurt you. Forgive God if you feel disappointed and let down by him.

When we forgive, we release bitterness and exchange it for sadness. That may not seem like an upgrade at first, but it is. As I said earlier, we can hold on to both sorrow and joy. You may feel sad about your past, but you'll finally be able to take hold of joy and thankfulness this Christmas. And I know from personal experience, it's an incredible gift from God.

PRAYER

God, forgiveness doesn't feel like what people deserve, but I know that you forgave me even though I was undeserving. Please give me the strength to let go of the bitterness I've been holding onto, so I can finally experience a deep sense of joy this Christmas. I am grateful for the gift of your son, Jesus, and that it's because of his sacrifice that I am fully forgiven and made new. Amen.

THIRTEEN

PSALM 63:1-5

God, you are my God; I eagerly seek you. I thirst for you; my body faints for you in a land that is dry, desolate, and without water. So I gaze on you in the sanctuary to see your strength and your glory. My lips will glorify you because your faithful love is better than life. So I will bless you as long as I live; at your name, I will lift up my hands. You satisfy me as with rich food; my mouth will praise you with joyful lips.

When you're experiencing a spiritual drought, do you run for the One who has living water? Or do you try to *do* more and *be* more to get yourself back on track?

My default is to be independent and self-sufficient. If there's a problem, I'll try to fix it first—no need to involve others by asking for help. And while that may be somewhat okay with other people, I end up really hurting myself when I do that with God.

It's interesting how in a season that is meant to celebrate Emmanuel (God with us), we get so busy and distracted with all the "doing" that we forget to *be with* God. When we forget to be with God, we end up feeling weak and malnourished—spiritually, emotionally, mentally, and physically.

All the loving, serving, and celebrating this month is good, but let's not forget to spend time with the One who matters most. This season shouldn't distract us from God, it should remind us to run after him, hungry for the only nourishment that truly satisfies us.

PRAYER

Jesus, thank you for being Emmanuel—God with us. Though this whole season is meant to celebrate your birth, sometimes I get so preoccupied with doing all the things that I forget to be with you—the One who matters most. Help me to find focus in all the busyness of life so that in everything I do, I glorify you. You are everything I need and more. Amen.

FOURTEEN

LUKE 1:28-30

And the angel came to her and said, "Greetings, favored woman! The Lord is with you." But she was deeply troubled by this statement, wondering what kind of greeting this could be. Then the angel told her: "Do not be afraid, Mary, for you have found favor with God.

I can't begin to imagine what it felt like to have the angel Gabriel in my presence, let alone to hear him tell me that I have found favor with God. No wonder Mary was a little taken aback!

Although we have not heard those words from Gabriel's mouth, we have been told that we are favored by God. We were told that truth when God sent his son, Jesus Christ, down from Heaven to take the punishment we deserved. Not only was our punishment taken from us, we were given the ultimate reward: a restored relationship with God himself—for all eternity.

When we struggle to see ourselves as favored by God, we start striving for the wrong things—like success, achievement, or recognition. While those things aren't bad in themselves, they are bad for us when our identities are tied to the things we do instead of our standing with God.

The Christmas season should be a time when we are reminded of God's favor, yet it often becomes a time for us to prove something to ourselves and others. This need to prove ourselves leaves us feeling empty. Instead, we can remind ourselves of just how loved we are, exactly as we are—which is how we find lasting joy and fulfillment.

PRAYER

Jesus, thank you for taking the punishment that should have been mine to bear. Because of your obedience to God and your sacrifice, I have been made fully and completely right with God. Please help me to remember how favored I am by my Father in Heaven so that I can stop all the striving. I have nothing to prove and only You to please. Amen.

FIFTEEN

COLOSSIANS 2:6-8

So then, just as you have received Christ Jesus as Lord, continue to live in him, being rooted and built up in him and established in the faith, just as you were taught, and overflowing with gratitude. Be careful that no one takes you captive through philosophy and empty deceit based on human tradition, based on the elements of the world, rather than Christ.

I'm not much for traditions. I like change, and I have a tendency to go in the opposite direction of the cultural norm. My heart is a little rebellious.

But in one area of my life specifically, I have seen this turn out to be a good thing. I have seen how my open-handed grasp of the way things are "always done" has given me a deep sense of freedom to do more of what Jesus wants me to do.

It's not a bad thing to have holiday traditions. I love going to church on Christmas Eve, opening presents on Christmas morning, and digging into the chocolate before I've even had a proper meal. Yet, sometimes we can get so wrapped up in our traditions—and the pressure to keep up with them—that we miss the whole point.

Traditions are fun and good. They can keep our families linked together and rooted in Christ. But if you're still struggling to find joy and meaning after our three weeks together, may I suggest letting go of how *you* think you should celebrate Christmas this year? Ask God how *he* wants to celebrate with you.

PRAYER

God, sometimes I get so wrapped up in all the fun things everyone else is doing that I forget to make it personal. I want this year to be different. I want to feel like I'm celebrating *with* you. Please quiet my soul and help me to hear your voice so you can guide me this Christmas. I'm so glad that you know me better than I know myself and that I can trust you to direct my days. I'm excited to celebrate your birth the way you want me to celebrate. Amen.

A FINAL NOTE...

It's almost Christmas, and before we both step into all that the holiday entails I want to remind you that **joy is possible**.

In our suffering.
In our struggle.
In our sorrow.

As the hymn says:

When peace like a river attendeth my way
When sorrows like sea billows roll
Whatever my lot, Thou hast taught me to say
It is well, it is well with my soul

Wishing you a Merry Christmas from my heart to yours.

—Taryn

ABOUT THE AUTHOR

Taryn Nergaard is the author of the *Reflective Bible Journals* and a life coach with a passion for helping people calm the chaos, quiet their souls, and find the clarity to move forward. Taryn lives in British Columbia, Canada with her husband and four kids. When she's not homeschooling or working, you'll find her enjoying a cup of coffee and a good book, or curled up on the couch binge watching her current favorite show.

@tarynnergaard
www.tarynnergaard.com

Does reading your Bible feel boring and difficult to apply to your life?

Are you unsure how to encourage your child's faith?

The *Reflective Bible Journals* for kids, teens, and adults help people of all ages connect with God through an intentional process of reflecting on and applying Scripture.

Visit reflectivebiblejournal.com to learn more.

www.ingramcontent.com/pod-product-compliance
Lightning Source LLC
Chambersburg PA
CBHW030917080526
44589CB00010B/349